CW00904194

Magic Spells
for
Mums

igloo

This book is published by Igloo Books Ltd
Henson Way, Telford Way Industrial Estate
Kettering, Northants, NN16 8PX
First published in 2005
© Copyright Smiling Faces Limited and Sevens Design 2004
All rights reserved
Printed in India

info@igloo-books.com

Warning: Not suitable for children
under 3 years, due to choking hazard.

This Magic Spells book is for mums everywhere. It is full of Magical Chants to bring a little well-deserved Magic to your lives, and show you just how much you mean to us! So take this book in your hand and read aloud the Spells inside. We can't guarantee your success, but we wish you every luck trying!

A Spell for a
Mother's Love

"For a mum who is loving and kind,
Who is always on my mind,
I send this Spell to show my love,
As words are simply not enough.
So hold this book and bring it close,
Imagine the scent of a mystical rose.
Then you will always feel the love in my heart,
Whenever we have to be apart."

A Spell for a Sweet and Powerful Mum

"Mums are like a Magical chocolatey treat.
They are kind, good and very sweet.
They make you happy when you feel sad,
And help you celebrate when you are glad.
And just like chocolate,
You can never get enough
Of such a sweet and perfect love."

A Spell for a Special Mum

"I know my mum worries about me,
And in her heart I will always be.
It makes me happy to know she cares,
To know with her my problems I can share.
So for her I wish lots of happiness and love,
Because hugs and cuddles just aren't enough."

A Spell for
a Magical Mum

"You have always been a Magical mum,
Who has known since I was young,
When I was happy, hurting or sad,
Who's held me tight when things were bad.
So deep inside this Chant doth dwell
A very strong and powerful Spell,
That will bring my mum happiness and cheer
For now, tomorrow and many a year."

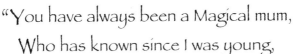

A Spell for
a Quiet Day

"I hate the smell of a stinky joss stick,
And scented candles that make you feel sick.
So I wish to relax the old-fashioned way,
With a cup of coffee and a quiet day.
No more strains, no more stress,
Just my kids treating me like a princess."

A Chilling
Out Spell

"As my life goes way too fast,
A Slowing Down Spell I shall cast.
So I wish for a comfy easy chair,
A glass of wine and snugly pyjamas to wear.
Then let time wait and stand still,
As I sit down to calmly chill."

A Spell to Relax

"As I sit down to rest for the first time today,
I wish for a Spell to ease my strains away.
Then as I ignore the time on the clock,
I wish for a huge box of chocs,
Which I can eat all on my own
In a small, cosy, child-free zone."

The Infamous Red Wine and Chocolate Spell

"Every moment is perfectly fine,
To conjure up chocolates and red wine.
Whether celebrating a special day,
Or drowning all my sorrows away.
So I wish for a nice glass of Bordeaux,
And a huge box of chocs tied with a pink bow."

A Spell for Manageable Hair

"I'm sick of my hair being a bird's nest
And never having time to look my best.
So with the power of Fairy Magic and luck,
Give me a permanent perfect look.
No more knots, no more frizz,
Thanks to a Magical sparkle, fizz, bang, whizz."

A Spell for a Thinner Waist

"Every time I look in my favourite mag,
It makes me frown and want to gag,
As on each page I am always faced
With women with hardly any waist.
So perhaps just for a day
This Spell can take my spare tyre away."

A Spell to Stop Getting Older

"All the years are rushing by,
And each new wrinkle makes me cry.
So I call upon the Powers of Youth
To make my wish become the truth.
Keep me young and ever so sprightly,
Raving and grooving daily and nightly."

A Lucky Spell

"To all the Sprites of luck and fate,
I request their presence to date.
Make me lucky,
Make me blessed,
Make my life the very best."

A Spell to Keep
a Bed Made

"I feel like my kids' personal slave,
Because their beds are never made.
So Alakazam, Alakazear,
Make this mess disappear.
Fluff the pillows.
Tuck in the sheet.
Hide the marks from their mucky feet."

A Spell to Make Food Slimming

"I call upon a Fairy's Magic Power
To fall on me in a shimmering shower.
Let me eat as much as I wish,
Emptying every delicious dish.
But as the next day doth come,
Keep me thin around my thighs and bum."

A Spell to
Empty the Bin

"Every day it's the same boring thing,
When I have to empty the blooming bin.
So make our rubbish disappear
As soon as the bin I get near.
No more half-naked trips at night,
That give my neighbours such a fright."

A Spell to Empty
the Wash Basket

"My washing machine is feeling the strain,
With the piles of clothes my children stain.
So I think it's time to give it a rest
From washing jumpers, jeans and vests.
So make their clothes stay Magically clean
With no stubborn stains or marks to be seen."

A Washing Up Spell

"As we don't have a dishwashing machine
It's time to get the kids to clean.
But it starts to become a real drag,
When I'm always being told I'm a nag.
So with a Magic daisy and yellow buttercup,
I wish to make them beg to wash up."

A Spell to
Get Rid of Ironing

""My ironing pile is now two storeys high,
And makes me want to break down and cry.
So make it all Magically disappear,
With no more steam, sweat or tears.
Then keep the pile permanently low,
So I don't wear out my poor elbow."

An Anti-Dropsies Spell

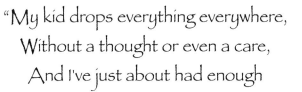

"My kid drops everything everywhere,
Without a thought or even a care,
And I've just about had enough
Of picking up clothes and personal stuff.
So I wish for a really powerful Spell
To make things rise from where they fell.
Make my home clean, make my home neat,
Not like some littered, scruffy old street."

A Spell to Stop
Nose Picking

"No adult understands or knows
A kid's obsession with their nose.
They are always picking
at their bogies and snot,
Tunnelling away to see what they've got.
So I wish for my kid to give it more thought,
And not entertain me with this sport."

An Anti-Fuddy Duddy Spell

"With the help of this powerful Spell,
I'd like me and my kids to really gel.
No more thinking I'm too old to understand
The lyrics and music of their favourite band,
Or that I think it's no big deal,
The way that life makes them feel."

A House Makeover Spell

"I'm addicted to DIY on my TV set,
But now I am starting to get upset,
Because it is time to confess
That the decor in my house is a real mess.
So with the help of a Magic paint tin
I want to change everything.
No more chintz, no more 80's chic –
Just a home that's contemporary and slick."

A Spell to Win the Lottery

"I play the lottery every week,
And now I wish for a winning streak,
To make my numbers a winning set,
To get me out of all my debt.
Then I'll spend it on a luxurious life
Without any grief, worries or strife."

A Spell for a Night Out

"Since our beautiful kids were born
I've stayed in from dusk till dawn.
So I command the Power of a Partying Sprite
To give me a fantastic, groovy night,
With no more worries and no more stress,
As we leave our kids with which we are blessed."

A Spell to Clear the Bathroom

"Now my child is a certain age,
And has hit the bathroom-hogging stage,
The rest of the family are starting to stink,
Because we can't get near the bath or sink.
So I ask the Fairy of all that's clean
To hurry along the preening routine."

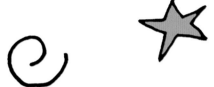

A Spell for
Peace and Quiet

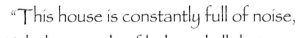

"This house is constantly full of noise,
With the sounds of kids and all their toys.
So when I next take time to sit,
Maybe things could be quiet for a bit.
So I wish for all the noise to cease,
And to fill the room with nothing but peace."

A Spell for a Happy Mother's Day

"As I read aloud this Magical Chant
Three Wishes shall the Fairies grant.
So first I wish for breakfast in bed,
And second an end to the housework I dread.
Finally I wish for my kids to play
Happily and quietly for just one day."